Also by Lynn Davies

The Bridge That Carries the Road

where sound pools

LYNN DAVIES

GOOSE LANE

Edited by Brian Bartlett.
Cover illustration by Getty Images.
Cover design by Julie Scriver.
Book design by Lisa Rousseau and Julie Scriver.
Printed in Canada.
10 9 8 7 6 5 4 3 2 1

Library and Archives Canada Cataloguing in Publication
Davies, Lynn, 1954-
Where sound pools / Lynn Davies.
Poems.
ISBN 0-86492-436-4
I. Title.
PS8557.A81968W44 2005 C811'.54 C2005-904197-8

Published with the financial support of the Canada Council for the Arts, the Government of Canada through the Book Publishing Industry Development Program, and the New Brunswick Culture and Sports Secretariat.

Goose Lane Editions
469 King Street
Fredericton, New Brunswick
CANADA E3B 1E5
www.gooselane.com

This book is for
John
Josie and Patrick

Contents

I With Knife And Basket

II Colliding With Light

Where Sound Pools

I With Knife And Basket

"Which direction are you headed?" he asked.

"North," said Stuart.

"North is nice," said the repairman. "I've always enjoyed going north. Of course, south-west is a fine direction, too."

"Yes, I suppose it is," said Stuart thoughtfully.

"And there's east," continued the repairman. "I once had an interesting experience on an easterly course. Do you want me to tell you about it?"

— from *Stuart Little,* by E.B. White

Testing

A sunflower by the wet, split-rail
fence, charcoal and lemon-yellow.
An ember minus heat and flicker
in the evening. Or a disembodied eye
staring back at me. Perhaps an ear —
frilled and attentive to the distant dogs
and crows, the crickets up close in the grass.

Or no, a microphone. A mike
that transmits to an alien ear
the cat bell, the kid on roller blades
snapping gum, tires on gravel,
the trembling aspen. Imagine hearing
all this for the first time. *Stay tuned*
I'd say, and walk away, whistling.

Vocation

With knife and basket, he goes to the woods,
takes years to write down the names of mushrooms

safe to eat. Begins with a touch of flesh
on the tip of his tongue, waits a day

or two for tingling, cramps, or swelling.
Then a tiny piece swallowed, sent to navigate

the twists and turns of the digestive system,
the nerves' back pools and eddies

pouring into the brain. All cells receptive.
Another piece, another wait, for pain

or visions. Once in a while he takes a day off
like the time he found a four-pound giant

puffball behind a barn down home.
Sliced it to lie in a frypan with butter.

A feast. He fed his friends. Out his window
he watches deer eat the honey mushrooms

growing on the old apple tree stumps.
He remembers hearing that hawks eat the eyebright

yellow in the fields. It strengthens their sight
for the slow-moving map below them.

For My Hiking Boots

We always kept walking
up Katadhin and Sagamook.
      Distant blue
misty hills from the top.
Knee-ache and water-envy
on the way down. Plural
descent. Even with you, boots,
I've never been as deft
on wet rocks as the dipper
we saw stride in and under
the Similkameen's flow,
      out again.

Boots, I could count on you
when trekking over beaches
giving way to my feet
and every storm that pummels
the coast. On the way out
  of a cove, I've passed
myself walking in. I say *ocean,*
my Finnish friend says *valtameri.*
Is a name a rest in a fluid world?
Matthew's Head. Kouchibouguac.

Even when we sleep, our planet's
in motion. Stillness impossible,
      although blue herons
are so convincing. You understood that,
the way you gravitated to my feet
eighteen years ago. Now thin-soled
and a minor constellation of holes.
Airy. Buoyant in the world

like the red salamander I saw
on the bottom back porch
step disappear into weeds
on delicate, three-toed feet.

Seedlings

Uneven as the tree line against the sky,
our twenty-four years together. The aspens
rarely still and the squirrels running trails
along the hardwood branches. Look
at the pictures. The backyard wedding.
We brandish an axe by my mother's
homemade wedding cake. My sister
dances with the red-nosed photographer
who will drive home and through his fence
thanks to my father's seasoned champagne.
Dead now: your parents, our brother-in-law,
my grandmother with her catnip wit.

We've managed a forest, although I can't say
how far it stretches, or identify all the movement
in it. Some silent places where a pig-eyed
  horned creature beds down. Days
  when trees seem to fall with intent.
We cut firewood, leave the dead spruce
standing for the pileated woodpecker I've heard
call at night (you've seen him with his mate.)

On the lawn you plant a young butternut,
ask me where to dig holes for the pear trees.
I consider, position the saplings where
they won't shade my flowers years from now.

Blueberry Island

Ping of berries in the old coffee pot.
Cedars and a white pine receive
the wind. Our canoe tied to a root
chafes the rocks, wants to go.

The Lip Family

You ask me of the strange flowers
I've sketched over the years.
Consider the Lip family —
a cantankerous, uneven group
if you ask me. The shiny petalled
almost black phanguylip
attracts lightning. I've seen a tree
overgrown with this vine struck
three times in a storm. I still think
Miranda wore those blooms
in her red hair on purpose. If you
can't win at love, you may as well
go out with a bang. Now if salesmen
or warlocks won't leave you alone,
put hoylip cuttings in a container
by your door. You need wood ashes,
a long handled knife and patience
to harvest hoys for these petite
yellow flowers spit
when approached and smell
worse than fishguts. Combine
hoys with coyote pee and you
have a concoction that'll empty
    a town square in minutes.
The wandering maddlelip looks
innocent enough, but try to sniff
a pink bloom and it mutters
what feels like obscenities.
I've seen plant-eating mammals
pull back as if stung. More subtle
are the tulips. Only in spring
do they drop their petals
in the first wind and rain.

I admire how they wear
their dishevelment, the pain
in the colour discarded, soon
devoured. Hardest to find
is the shy taylip. Climb a tree
at night and you might spot
its glow: the most exquisite
scented flower of any colour,
often in abandoned nests.
Never pick one. A lead-heavy
hand and burning fingers for years
always at night. Which is why
I stay close to home now
and welcome your letters. The birds
come daily and I sketch them too.
Some rest in the hand I extend,
    my arm like the branch
I've seen dip with a bird's arrival, lift
    when the body chooses air.

How to Cut Water

It's not easy. First you find water spread out like a rug. Let it congeal, grow thick, and pass into hardness. Then tie knives to your feet, one blade per foot, and push off from the boards. Forget what you need for the chili you plan to make this evening, push the memory of last spring's lilacs away. These thoughts will draw your skate's tip to the crack others glide over or worse, pull you down on the soft spots. But I've seen blades take to the air, then descend for the incision. You must learn the weight of empathy, to align your body with cold. Try a shrew's tunnel under snow or the tiny ice moonlets circling Saturn. Many cuts have never been catalogued. But it's possible to carry water away in pieces; the loss of shape beginning as you hold a slice close to your body on the way home.

Songs of the Parking Lot Attendant

1

Almost everything I know
comes from what's left
behind. What I hear
as they walk or drive
in and out. I am the hour
hand of their days.

2

Some people yak
like a whipper-snipper.
Others dismiss the day,
a card hand tossed out quickly.

Unlike the storytellers, so generous
with anecdote and embellishment,
comrade Time always on their side.
The singers, the whistlers.
Even the volume of their car radios
as they drive away
stays with me.

3

Each voice, a piece of fabric
in the quilt that covers me at night.
Some tongues wistful as silk,
between Emma and the weather
i lost sleep this summer

The man to his dog,
when my time comes give away my pants
and burn the rest of me

Awake under a quilt crazy with scraps
of old ties — *tired of chasing*
garbage can lids — jeans,
nightgowns.

my best breakfast
is a whistle dog
with gravy on the fries

My hand travels the cottons, the cross-stitching,
tries to calm an ocean. Finds
the odd sequin. Trails of bubbles.

The soft corduroy pieces.
november clover
i like november clover
because it hangs on

4

In my parking lot
the lines and right-angled corners
painted white and straight
are a kind of cutlery tray,
all utensils given a place.
Tidier than tying your fly-bitten,
tail-flicking horse to a hitching post.

When my lot's empty
I practise walking those lines. I might
need the extra balance someday.

I've heard the guy who walks
lonely down the railway tracks sing
I walk the line
because you're mine.
Sounds like he's going somewhere.

I walk my lines at night
and backwards. Try it. Up on your toes,
then lower your heel and hope it finds
the line too. Now your other foot nudges
the back of your wide-awake heel. Sometimes
I've imagined the poise
of a third leg and foot. Trust yourself
in the dark on a faded line. A siren
or a cell phone is enough to push you off

and open every old wound
in your body. There are so many ways
to fall, the pavement unforgiving.

5

Aah, the storytellers. Once
a man called her Vanessa,
and she took it the way some people
read shooting stars.

"Why'd you quit wrestling," he asked. "I loved
watching you drop that Two-Ton Tessa
like a truck backing up to dump its load
of broken concrete." Of course she went to lunch

with him, wanting to know more
about who she was supposed to be.
His book, *Fringe Occupations,*
was coming along; he asked
questions about the wrestling circuit.

She told him, one Christmas Eve
the notorious Gory Greta had tossed her so hard
she'd suffered concussion and enough amnesia
to rob her of the five memory-packed years
leading up to that event.
"For all I know," she said
"Vanessa might not be my name." If writing
something down is an act of faith
then he believed her. Asked her
for Vanessa — recalls she composed on the spot.
She surprised herself with details of recovery
and another life. As if, for the first time,
she saw people out walking their dogs at night,
the little blue light at the Bowlarama,
her love like a late spring tulip, petals unhinging.

"If you," he said, "can start over again,
not even sure who you are, why can't I?"
You're The Muscle In My Heart is the song
he wrote for her before leaving town
with someone called Breanne.

Maybe a cat follows her home,
purrs while drinking the water
she's poured in a bowl. Cleans
its tabby body in her favourite
chair. She names the cat
Entanglement.

6

I sweep my lot when it's empty.
Where puddles collect, pebbles drift.
If I lie down, my horizons
multiply in blades of grass
and the edge of a highrise.

It's a big floor I sweep, the swish
lulling as a drink before bed. Dust storms
and wrappers. Bottles, the odd condom.
  I am a local wind
  on the surface.

An astrolabe could lie below, well-
preserved, lost on a long carry.
Or deeper, a marsh-soaked mother
  holding her child. Or maybe

I take money on top of the biggest
undiscovered oil well on the continent.
Waiting to seep through a crack
on a day my eyes water from the sun
glinting off the rows of parked metal and glass.

How quickly the wild grasses could take over
this lot. Once, while sweeping, I found a book,
    Field Guide To The Butterflies.
Waiting for sleep, I repeat my favourite line:

the great bird-winged butterflies of the Old World

the great bird-winged butterflies of the Old World

7

I listen for other winds too. Breath
in a bottle, in a body, round a blade of grass.
The 18-wheelers pulling
their winds behind them. How the weather settles
when the motor dies.

Voice is breeze in a labyrinth.

8

I hear you too, frog
  loud and clear
in my parking lot
  at dusk.

Squash Flowers

My son picks the flowers
  off the squash vine
rambling over the lawn, floppy
yellow petals veined green.

He weights a blossom
with a penny. Floats it
in a deep glass vase.
Tendrils descend — fish,

feelers probing new waters.
He leans another in a shallow
brown bowl. Blown in,
  exhausted, simply

exhausted, and the bowl's
painted windmill steadily
works the air. The third
  bristles with pollen

in a crimson bowl. More
golden than the others,
alert to the meticulous
clock, the marauding flies,

the papers on the table.
Like the full moon's
gaze in the afternoon sky.
A fledgling's first dive.

Vows of Silence

One late summer, we tied notes to bushes,
chalked messages on pavement. Trailed stones
to a broken mirror at the edge of the woods.
Two flashes meant *approaching the fort,*
pray for me. One flash: *heard all,*
be back soon. Delicious when it worked.

After days of this, the first leaf to fall
on the dog kennel took on significance.
Who was behind the new cracks in the road,
the dead bumblebee on the second step?

A candle in a window meant *I will be silent*
in my dreams tonight. This, we discovered,
was beyond our control. We wrote down
what we said in our dreams, packed the papers
into a blue tin box, buried
our insistent voices in a backyard.

Frosty Porch Blues

Cat on the porch, I know you hear the wind
 in the leaves on the ground.
Another cold-paw season coming
 and nowhere to walk

except the paths I'll shovel to the woodpile,
 the road, and for you.
Hey cat, if a train ever comes through
 this damn town,

we'll hop it, the rails warming up, rolling
 us south together.
Winter's a big room for worries, cat.
 How to pay the bills,

dry boots out in time, will the roads disappear
 again tomorrow?
Ice in your water bowl and my knees, days
 and days inside.

Hey cat, would you consider wings?
 Rare birds, you and I,
above the trees already bare and days
 going up in smoke.

We could follow the wild geese south,
 mess up their V.
No worries cat, nothing to fall into
 but the sky.

Girl with Shell

The girl cups the shell in her hands to her ear,
head bent. Her ear so like the vessel in shape

and passage. Once again the ocean inside
speaks of where the shell comes from, a place

in the world she believes impossible to find.
She notices how a deep breath is amplified,

the shell willing to share her geography too.
How still she stands on the ocean's floor.

Years later she will listen, the sound nothing
but the blood roaring in her head, reclaiming her.

The dunes and the sea in the shell are a coastline
she will recognize inside her, more water than land.

Calling My Son Home, I Remember

Outside after dinner in early October,
    the breath of the beast
called dusk filling ditches. We avoided

back fields and unfinished houses
    where during the day
we'd walk through walls, elope, bury

bodies in basements. But now birch bark
    and what we called
snake berries gleamed eyeball white,

the berries *pop* under our feet precise
    as the shots meant
to scare off coyotes. Crickets still sang.

Our voices ricocheted off enclosures
    and pavement as we waited
for the back porch lights to flick on.

Early October

The old round hills in the tide lines.
Beyond the beach, the dew on the asters
reminds me of a friend. Autumn rain
speckling her glasses, hiding her eyes.

The Map Maker

She crosses the valley of dry thunder
storms where the people never eat meat
killed by lightning. She relies on a map
of pictures: a boy riding his buffalo home,
wild mushrooms under pine trees, a coffin,
a comb, and five holy mountains. She chooses
to stay on the street of the candle-makers,
among people who honour stolen hours.
Near the old man who would not
be knocked down by fierce winds, fire,
and poor investments. She tries to draw
a map for travel through winter. How many
ways to vary white? Each snowflake
adds to silence but cannot cover the names
she will give to places. Lost — you
can always walk towards the name.

Moss Roses in a Vase

So many pictures began
for him in the city streets,
parks, and mirrored bars.
At the train station
or bull fights. Now
in bed with syphilis,

his left foot amputated,
he paints things set down
for a moment or arranged
to stay put for awhile —
peonies, a brioche, a lemon.

The glass vase and water
blur the cut stems and leaves
schooling like fish. He paints
the pink to reddish-brown
  moss roses in petal
  after alarming petal

  and light. As if
they dream their time
in the ground. Spade-
clunk on a rock, wood
smoke, water drawn
from a shallow well.

Approaching Vespers

Order for the eye in the long elm boulevard
and its timely shade, the trimmed cedar,
rough spruce in parallel rows.
Beyond the abbey, the roads cut grids
under a sky so big I wonder if it'll fall

like a blanket or in pieces. Two magpies
chase a cat past Mary in her shrine. Bells
call the monks to their late afternoon prayers.
Timing and breath for a hundred years
on this square of prairie. Feet mulling the gravel,

we bring our histories too. One side chants,
the other responds. Brothers industrious
as ants working the peony buds. My untrained
ear, surprised at the single chanter. Later, the owlet,
ookpik-fat and whistling on the ground.

The Time of Novels

In my teens, in my bedroom,
I devoured full novels in days.
Could smell the fires burning
on Egdon Heath. Wished Merlin
could turn me, too, into a fish
or a goose for the sake of a sound
education. Plot after flowing plot

until the boy I'd loved for a year
took off like a fish hawk. Then
books were heavy and the word
Michelangelo too long. I reread
sentences for the sounds I'd missed
as if loss could be a puzzle on a page.

I still plod through books. Passages
remulled, looking behind me,
parting lines like blades of grass.
The art of wholeness possible
but seamless as evaporation, fine-
tuned as rain speckling the pavement.

Driving West on the 116

I turn off the old highway at Harcourt
over the railway tracks, past the white
cross and the man selling moosehorns.
Hard to believe that a moose at home
in these bogs could be tricked by a man
blowing through coiled birchbark.
No traffic to speak of, just bush,
the odd sign, and cattails.

Through Ghost Hollow, over the bridge
at Castaway Creek. The metal potholes
and fading goldenrod. Once by the road,
a bear — and I remember the lines from Stegner.
. . . *so they aimed themselves toward Leadville*
through the notch of a horse's ears. Home
the other side of Mosquito Pass with horses
so worn out one dies before the end

    of the trail. I listen to Bach,
his Brandenburg concertos, confident
as the water curving blue through the early
autumn valley. This road I follow
    is a notch and the bush
could be the green brindled ears
of something we can't see to name.

Young Bassoonist

Despite the audience,
a fleet of music stands,
violin bows fumbled,
    dropped —
the orchestra begins.
In the front row,
some kids stiff
as cold licorice.
Others at home
in a collaboration
intricate as a woodpile.

Perhaps a lost passage,
some mangled notes
I rarely notice.
I admire these
rough beginnings, the light
on their forearms, my
daughter's foot tapping

time and her slow pull
on her cello's bow
beside the boy
with the bassoon.
Cheeks puffed, lips
clamped to a short
hookah, his arms
around a huge, black
tube. On the way
home she says

I don't know how
he played, he barely
had time to breathe

February

I slice grapefruit,
oranges, lemons,
inflame tiny holes
in my parchment hands.

Seeds pile like debris
along a shoreline after
wind. The overnight
soak in water to soften

the thick-skinned fruit.
Colours deepen in the
long boil, calendulas
in a pot. Every window

steamed shut, sugar
sinks slow as ice.

In jars, the rinds
curl like entrails
waiting to be read.
In tonight's sky

floats a half moon
but no amount of
tree-stirring, wind-boiling
will soften its skin.

The Banana Blues

How many bananas go black every
        day in this country?
Clown grins losing their grip
        on counters, in lunchbags.

Slightly phallic for the restless, almost
        always on sale,
rock-hard and green. My mother still
        says to me *never*

throw out old gum, pickle juice,
        or rusty bananas.
So I mix up more damn 'ana bread
        when John says

let me dig a hole in the backyard
        and bury the ones
        you froze last year.

Insomniacs, why count sheep when you
        can count bananas?
Life's little boomerangs buried
        en masse.

Three Pumpkins

We have company. Three carved pumpkins
on the table, their insides dark. One
is a connoisseur of dungeons, he might
offer you rat tails from his dress coat pocket.
The second waits with missing teeth
and centipede scars for the pipes to start,
she wants to dance. The third's amoebic
mouth releases a wind, it's a mask
to wear when hungry. I lift a stem
to light a candle, look in to see the world
through pumpkin eyes. Bottom of the ocean
black, any sound taking hours
to sink to the silty floor. What's left
of the memory of germination. An informal
lobotomy, thanks to a kitchen knife,
a bowl, and a hand reaching in
for the first tug at flesh and seeds.

Quartet

Try to stay calm before the empty chairs
and music stands in the pre-performance
silence; in an old round church with a
sloping floor and stained glass windows

bright as the innards of a sheep I once
saw cut open. They begin with Handel
and the cello is the wood intact and tonal
under the snow outside. And all of them,

reaching with bows on strings are tree
tips against the sky. From the hilltop
the firs flow through the hardwoods
and the rising sap is a new red current

stretching north to Stanley. They would
not seem out of time or place in a forest
clearing muffled with over-sized snowflakes
in no hurry to reach the warming earth.

I won't place deer or a bobcat
at the edge of the trees drawn by sound.
I'll put myself, cold, probably lost,
bringing fire so they'll keep on playing.

Hemlock

The old hemlock blew down last winter.
Who could decipher what's written in the scrolls
rolled and stacked to dry in the sun and wind?
They spit and crackle in the stove.

Falling Angels

The first one is headless and falls
through the dusk, wing-chunks big
as its pearly body. A newspaper.
Or sky-debris, you say, until hours
or years later with no forewarning
shadow to skim the ground, another
airborne being in pieces, back
of its wings blue and falling
into the cherry blossoms. Over time
  you suspect that what you see
of angels depends on what they
fall through or against. The ones
in front of a building about to buckle
under the wrecking ball or winged figures
around a person blown to bits, these
are the angels hardest to see. Some fall
in pairs, wear flames. You've dreamed
of them talking to gravity, giving it features
and a muscled forearm. The grackles
in the trees, so like pieces of something
once bigger, they too watch for impact:
a hairline crack in pavement, flattened grass.

The Dwarf

Grave as drought, he endured days
of sand. No fits of rage or ego, not
like those canyon-people who deserted
my friend mid-journey. Hard at first
not to stare at the tentacles, the long
thinning earlobes hanging to his waist,
burgundy and slim as bean tendrils.
                                        More hearing?
Maybe. I've seen him lie down and place
those filaments on the ground. Bird's feet
or a stethoscope. In the treed valleys
when I still enjoyed deep sleep, I dreamt
I cut my finger on the horizon line. He
thought dreaming oppressive.
    When dwarves rest, the nights
    like clear water fill us up.
We travelled into country where trees
gave up. Nothing but sand and the shapes
it assumed that day. Our first clues:
a boot, a bench, three steps
leading nowhere. Closer, the lean
of buildings and airy doorways, all coming
    and going gone except for lizards
or the tracks of jackals. The dwarf chose
a room so full of sand it raised his sleep
close to the ceiling. A *sound-room* he said
and almost smiled. He was remembering
underground chambers where sound
pools long before any creature
hears it. I think that's why
they're so serious. They hear
what's beyond us and stop
to answer our questions.

Yes, it's strange, and no,
I can't tell you his name. Dwarves
don't like their names passed
among strangers, and one stranger
is enough for a dwarf. He was a friend,
comfortable underground yet patient
in territory known for its heat
and light, hostile unless you wear scales
or hunt in packs. He led me through
that country and never complained.

Up the E6

Early May and we headed north into Scandinavia,
roadside waits that imprinted barns and place names
in my head for years. *Trondheim. Ringebu.*
A driver's silence. They were used to this, one
Norwegian mile measuring ten kilometres.
The cold that toughens people kept me awake
in empty campgrounds. If a troll is still out
at sunrise, he'll explode, and every seven years
thousands of lemmings crawl under and over
everything, including tents. I heard the sparrows
in our cooking pots, pecking at leftovers.

The long haul truck driver stopped
so we could stand on the Arctic circle.
Narvik. Moen i Malselv. One road.
Sometimes it gave way to boats
and people coming together to cross fjords.
A man said he couldn't understand the country
we were going to. What fills all that space?
Forest and the odd farm here and there.

What we found was light, that the sun
never gives up on silence. Even at midnight,
a sky streaked pink and tangerine
trying to illuminate private trees and empty
potato cellars, an old German bunker
and the bones of a lamb. Something hidden
and inarticulate but brighter as the summer
wore on, big as the adult world
when I was small and looked up at people.
Thought I'll never get there, I'll never arrive.

II Colliding with Light

. . . and Serafina Pekkala flew away on her cloud-pine branch over the reeds, over the marshes, over the mudflats and the beach, and over the sea, until Mary could see her no more.

— from *The Amber Spyglass,* by Philip Pullman

Time after Time

When you stop
to rest, a crow
flies away
with your watch.
Only the breeze
on your white-lined
wrist.

You make it home
with your bag of
pre-peeled, pre-washed
carrots, a pragmatic
purchase so you can
make an elaborate
dessert or watch
ice fishing on TV.

A guest may assume
you scraped and washed
the roots in the sun pouring
through the kitchen window,
music turned down low.

As images do, these
invite more. She sees
you bent over the first
thinning of carrots
in the 13th century
under the sign of Gemini.

You sprinkle chives
on the barely-tender carrots
in a blue bowl, smell
rain from the northeast.
Think of time bright
 as spoons and tinfoil
in a moss-lined nest.

The Coppermine Trail

By late summer the stream runs dry,
becomes an old road worn smooth
by sandalled feet and donkeys pulling
stone-wheeled carts. What beckons

this embellishment? Isn't it enough
to study the rocks, moss, and debris,
the steps of gravel under the deadfall
still leafing, to imagine the sure

tone of water to pools, the minnows,
racoon paws, and evaporation? Every
ledge carouses with depth and the sky,
where water regathers to tap rocks

and ferns, their undersides
speckled with spores. This old
fertility, water in a tin cup,
a deep place in a stream.

After Halftime

No fixed address for lightning. A tree here,
a chimney there, or the woman two provinces over,
her clothes blackened, reciting the multiplication
tables to clear the noise from her head.
And last week, just down the hill,
the girl running onto the soccer field
with her teammates. Ahead in the finals,
any storm a rumble, a rumour. One stray
   but deft bolt out of the blue and life
is rearranged in a body in seconds, friends
and families watching. Memory finds a home
in our stories and random lightning too. Is it
true what the scientists say? That these storms
favour the Alberta foothills, and in the winter
an ocean south of Sable Island. Today
in this field by the school, masses
of white clover gather like clouds
where the girl collided with light.

Geography

A swallowtail butterfly
lies in my hand, yellow
wings webbed with black.
On the lower wing's edge,
a new moon and a finger
of land. Like the one I
drew in school and coloured
green, then blue around
its three shores: *peninsula.*
A new word applied to the stones
I'd been pouring in puddles
for years. Give me time
and I'd find a peninsula
in tidal brown waters or deep
sea green. I'd sit on its point,
the flat rocks and wind, and
when the weather turned
I'd run back to the continent
still attached. Unlike the island
with trees, a beach, and a wisp
of smoke alone in the blue
I spread on the rest of the page.

Collision

We drive through dusk, the trees wet
from the day's rain. A maple glows
stoplight red and my daughter sings
with the radio, the one about the car crash
and the last kiss. How he'll be good so
he can see her in heaven. Rare frogs

in the shallows, these are the yellows,
and I sing too. I remember these lines,
the idea of loyalty staying buoyant
in someone a comfort. Nearly a promise
thanks to lyrics at dances, on our way
home, in our bedrooms. Up ahead,

newt-orange foliage, almost
unearthly. I want to tell her that leaves
fall like we do. The reds first, in a yes-
to-the-wind last fling. On a day so calm
we might hear a leaf land, brief
gorgeous trim for the balsam fir.

Germination

With potatoes, all the action's underground.
That's how she begins. She's full of stories,
some tall and rambly as a mountain range.
But I like this one. Her obsession with size,
the burly vines, the slow granular orange
  deepening everyday in her garden.
She grew them huge as an affirmation. Big
is bold and bountiful, weight is all
about confidence. Anyway,

one day she goes out to look at her crop
and she thinks she hears a child crying.
Muffled, as if from inside a box.
She checks the bushes, the chard, the raspberries —
no injured animal, no runaway kid
like Josh Oates found in his climbing bean
teepee midsummer. She wonders
if she's having a psychic growth spurt,
sure now the wailing comes
from inside a pumpkin the size
of a small doghouse. Her biggest,
her finest, about 432
pies of fresh pumpkin.

She takes out her army knife. Will the racket stop
if she breaks the vine? But the crying's awful
childlike. Could it be a pumpkin fever,
another damn virus to catch? She cuts the vine.
Renewed wailing and her dog goes nuts,
whining and trying to dig at the thing.
So she cuts out the stemmed top,
looks inside. Finds the baby,
orange with pulp and gumming seeds.

You laugh. I did too. The facts
of life cloaked, a folksy twist
on immaculate conception. Not that he's
any saint, that kid. But don't you love
the details? She never changes them.
And ever since we lost our lights,
I admit I crave stories —
                                        but let me
finish. She could ignore crows
and yowling cats but not a baby crying
loneliness and hunger. Those were the days
when too many were found near-dead
in dumpsters or the stinking harbour. She cut
the hole bigger, pulled the child out.

She jokes about it. Stuck to leaf lettuce
and summer savory for a long time. Jumpy
for awhile, afraid of what she might hear
from any oversized veggie thriving
in a patch of soil. But the boy cured her of that.
One blue eye, one green eye, and hair
the colour . . . well, you know, you've seen him.
A talker right from the start and he loved
her stories. A gifted mimic too —
a junco, a creaky tree, the whirr
of a junebug: he can utter
any sound close to the earth.

The Crossing Season

If you cross the river just before the full moon,
the tides force the crack off Miser's Island
open, where my grandmother's horse broke through
years ago. Now the frosty morning crossings
take ten minutes, unless your front
wheels find open water. Then
the wobble-leg trek to shore. Some people
say the ice road season isn't
as long as it used to be. No shortcuts
to heaven, they say too, but I crave the ones
into town. Mid-river, my seatbelt undone
and my door open, I rehearse the osprey's
feet-first plunge and take off. Pray
for the pure blue ice — or black will do.

Composing Winter

Then consider in your own mind how much work you can do in a day; for whatever you plaster you ought to finish up. It is true that sometimes in winter, in damp weather, working on a stone wall, the plaster will occasionally keep fresh until the next day; but do not delay if you can help it, because working on the fresh plaster, that is, that day's, is the strongest tempera and the best and most delightful kind of work.

— from *Il Libra dell' Arte* (1390), by Cennino d'Andrea Cennini, translated by Daniel V. Thompson, Jr.

When your back is turned to meals,
when you're asleep, more snow falls.
You can't trust the memory of leaves.

The hardwoods wear white auras
and the deer come to eat the frozen apples
still hanging in our gardens.

Only the V is real. Where the branch
parts from the trunk to hold the snow
neither wind nor sun can disturb.

You watch evergreen become everwhite.
How driveways fill up again. Fences
disappear. Hills defy cars.

Tunnels are a way of life. My children
burrow into snowbanks, carve out rooms
they talk of heating with fire.

The one rule: always dig towards a friend.
A shovel's distant tap-tap
the only bearing for those cocooned

in snow's rare light. The funnelled shout
when, at last, a boot or wooden spoon
breaks through. I remember all this,

watching them look out the kitchen window
at their small, dark entrance. They know
how it grows into a bigger space.

At night, the snow angels gossip
under the bird feeders where they've seen
other winged things gather by day.

They cannot go far, they belong to the bodies
of the children who made them. They have no real names.
It's "hey angel" or "what happened to your wing?"

What an angel remembers of creation:
snow-sound and the weight of shadow after
the child rises. "Weren't you made beside me?"

We think they melt to animate the snowdrops.
But a child sees a snowy owl drift over a field
and thinks, oh! my angel, it flies away after all.

Fresh snow becomes for me the plaster
wet and ready for the hand holding
a fine bristle brush dipped in verdaccio,

first of the flesh colours. A day's work —
perhaps a face, or two irate camels.
Giotto, the storyteller. Hands reaching

for a child. The curiosity of an ox. Evening
was the best time to carry the willow to the baker.
The day's bread done, he'd bake the sticks

into charcoal for drawing. Giotto's figures
first sketched on paper, perspective considered,
these are the shadows of trees on snow.

We can't imagine the lives of birds rendered
in frescoes. St. Francis under a tree, his hands
fine-boned as the birds who stop to listen.

The other monk Giotto includes cannot
believe what he sees. Birds stilled by syllable
when Francis calls to them. A chittering flock,

now a feathered ear. Except for the ghostly doves,
it's hard to identify the fading birds. Eliminate
the obvious: no crows or herons. Maybe painted

birds fly away too, their withdrawal a slow
takeoff into the frescoe's blue hills. Or out
the church door, looking for the likeness of trees.

I know the deer forage our yard at night,
their trails like veins in a leaf.
Following the edge of the forest

and what's visible of the fence to our young
pear trees, their succulent tips.
Where do they go when the snow

lies thigh-deep and crusty
after two days of ice pellets?
We hack out a path to the woodpile,

wonder at last night's thunder and lightning,
stranger than summer hail. Redpolls flock
to the feeders, our cats test the top of the snow.

The weight of it. Families gather on roofs
to push the snow off. Cats perch
on the pile ploughed high under

the feeders. They wait for more than seed
to fall. My son navigates the rink on skates
with a stick and shrewd grace. And I, as the goalie,

on my barracuda blades collapsed on the ice
with card house finality. The weight of the cast
on my arm. How the ice-caked trees crackle.

The hollow-boned birds sing anyway.
Scraps of empty bellies in frozen trees.
Wood splits easily, it's that cold.

Only Lazarus is dressed for winter.
Bound in strips of linen, his head covered,
his face bleached from four days in a cave

closed with a stone. The voice he heard
immediate as a tree snapping in the cold,
"Lazarus, come out." Or distant

as the coyote I'm not sure called from outside
or in my sleep. Never the doubter, Lazarus
leaves his tomb for fresh air and his friends

unbinding him. Giotto paints his eyes closed.
Surprised at the weight of blood mapping his body.
Hands numb, feet slow to move through days.

Loneliness is an ice-encased leaf
and fear burns like a grassfire. This
is why Giotto paints grieving angels.

Their gowns fluttering into a blue
pounded and crushed from lapis lazuli,
most valued of pigments. Is there clarity

in the holes we don't dig for ourselves?
New snow and the car on black ice,
the river rising by the minute. Some nights

the best we can do is applaud a child
with a flashlight and a snow tunnel's glow.
A fire by the lake we skate on.

March

Soprano coyotes in the valley again.
Deer on the run or the new moon's trail?
I turn on the bathroom light: a ladybug
walks the rim of the water glass.

Breaking Trail

Stop for breath and the coyote prints,
the shrew's intricate cross-hatching
in last night's new snow. Every halt
a junction: the ski tracks and the pole's
pock marks behind me. Ahead,
the abandoned white road, snowflakes
still intact after their fall.

I find the trail I made earlier
beginning to ice over. Push off
to glide through tree shadows
on a track that glistens. My flight
certain as the rustling beech leaves
that will fall, then gather
in the deer tracks enlarged by the sun.

The Bowhead Whale

A woman walks
on the thick sea ice,
walks with the wind,
knows a clear sky
will darken over the
open water. She sits
on a slab of ice, spots
a bowhead resting
on its back in the sea
opening up around her.
She sings.

50 to 60 feet long, one third
of that body is head. Thick-
skinned, streamlined, reinforced
with cartilage to ram
through ice for air.

She sings to stay awake,
to push the cold away. Slips.
Sees her ice slab
overhead and bright
in the darkness,
her body heat rising
in bubbles. When
does she close her eyes?

Pinhole ears. But the bones
in its head and jaw receive
whatever sounds water
and ice send. Chirping beluga
forwarded to the middle ear.
Or the moan of another bowhead
  a two or three
  day swim away.

Deep into the whale she moves,
cocooned in blubber thick
as the length of her arm.
Lulled by its fluke-driven,
forward movement, easy
  roll and descent.
  Heart's drum
  slowing down.

No dorsal fin on its broad back,
free to swim beneath ice
in water so cold we'd die
  in two minutes.

She lights a fire.
The bowhead surfaces,
opens its jaws, and the men
who see the smoke hunt
the whale. Deliver her,
the whale's blood melting
  holes in the ice.

In spring, bowhead whales
follow the open water leads
to the Beaufort Sea. Slow moving,
60 ton islands, their four chambered
    stomachs empty.

If you doubt her story,
    she'll tell you
the whale carries her
for a day and a night. Or
is it two? Or three? Spits
her out into the slush close
to the shore fast ice. Walks
until she finds people
who live behind walls
of driftwood and whale ribs,
the sod roofs held up
by jawbone beams.

Someone has seen a bowhead
breach 57 times in an hour
and a half. Courtship? Slapping
 parasites off its body? Noise
for nearby whales?

Or she might tell you she
slumps in the whale's belly
or more likely the mouth, discovers
a man and his dog team there too.
He lights a moss-wick lantern,
gives her food. They sing.
The dogs howl. The whale
answers and they wake up
at the water's edge. If she
knows you're lost, she'll
add their child who lives
in a city to the south. Who
sings this story when driving
under a river in a well-lit tunnel.

Bowhead sounds are described
as simple or complex moans
at low frequencies. Listen:
the origins of bass. Taking its
time, weighted as the water
these whales displace.

Chalice Tree

In the evergreens, the old beech tree
spreads giant limbs to the sky.
Invites light, holds more than snow.
Who will fill this cup?

Waiting Room

I'm waiting for my son's teeth to be cleaned
and examined, the walls of the room a tranquil
blue-grey and plum. Out the window
I see the green shingles of an old house,
the eaves crammed with icicles, drops
caught in the act of dripping. And I hope
that a creature with fangs that long
and polished might be charmed with a song,
a trick of landscape, or something shiny.
The wind picks up yesterday's snow.
Could it be the dandruff of Giant George
floating over our town again? The same
  George who once upon a time
honoured gravity — but this story flounders
when the man in dark glasses, sniffing
and pulling up his socks two seats down,
looks at me, then out the window
where the wind gusts so hard the house
next door disappears. We see sun specs on flakes
so turbulent, I know we're moving, this little
carpeted room coming in for a landing.

Dodging the Melt

The push through old snow
past slush and the new browns
in the upturned roots of toppled trees,
rocks and hummocks poking through.

Deer droppings everywhere.
The stops to rewax, remove clothes,
watch crows on the move. The tug
then glide of my skis from sun

to shade, the worn-down snow
crystals change that fast.
Even a clump of pussywillows.
It's the tail end of winter I ski,

past the deep woods snow
littered with twigs and needles
along the sides of the once solid
trail, now pooling and running away.

The Witch's Boots

A witch chases my son into copper
hills on the last day of his twelfth
year. I trail her into the tunnel
he crawls down, cat-like and scared.
If I pull off her boots, run back
into daylight, push my feet in —

her spell will fade as the sun
sets. When I leave the cave
carrying her dusty boots,
she gives me concrete arms
and a metal rod for a spine.
Boulder-feet and the jaw
set so I can't call to the boy
in the air above *go home*
keep stones under your pillow

Dusk in my granite head for years,
the world a plane's drone. A distant
airfield. When my children find me,
I see their eyes are still oceans,
but busy with cargo, haunted by rumours
of benign lights and rough amethyst.

Loon Chat

The loon's long call is a lost
train. You might see its lights
if you look between the hills
and stars. Okay, let's be more

grounded. This bird of dense
bones swims otter-like among
the water lily stems. Hears
the rain below and translates *all*

bodies of water begin small.
Or says to its mate or child
fishing's good today. Loon-
chat, that's all these calls are.

And the frogs, guttural and happy
in the mud, wonder why the opera
begins again. Croak *elitists, elitists.*
But sometimes they agree loon-

yodels do break up the nights
growing longer and creatures
that lonely really need to hear
their echoes off the treeless cliff.

Grey

The world begins
in grey. The clouds
and waking hardwoods.

The river rises
to cover our trail
and climb the trees.

A garden of limbs
and red-winged
blackbirds.

This morning's first
words on the radio -
the upper valley.

I'd wear grey
and go there.
All day I've kept

those words free
of attachments. No
warning, no praise.

Just dusk, myself,
and the deer. On the trail
beginning to dry out.

For Appetite

On the lawn lies the faded sunflower head
abandoned by the squirrel. A hummingbird
rests, then drinks from our apricot-petalled
hollyhock. Our belled white cat
has not come home for three days.
We hear of the bobcat sightings,
the likely gang of young coyotes
looking for new territory, how a fox
will bury its kill to eat it later. A friend
complains of the crows cawing her awake
every morning, heading for their favourite
dumpster. The fishermen call this time of year
the August Darks. No moon, and the herring
swim close to the shore, get caught in the weirs.
I remember the butterfly in her mouth. The winter
of beheaded redpolls. She loves to sit
at the edge of things — the forest, a lake,
a puddle will do. Days fade early now.
Often I hear a bell but it's always a cricket,
more high-pitched, long-winded than the rest.

Acknowledgements

Thanks to the editors where some of these poems were first printed or broadcast: *The Fiddlehead, The Malahat Review, Poets Premiere* on CBC Radio. Also the anthologies *Why I Sing the Blues, An Orange from Portugal, Listening with the Ear of the Heart, Coastlines.*

For help in revising many of these poems, thanks to Sue Goyette, Ross Leckie, Anne Simpson, John Steffler, and the Icehouse Poetry Group. A huge thanks to Brian Bartlett for his editorial eyes and ears, and his sense of humour. Thanks again to John McConnell for the time to write and for his faith in the process.

I'm grateful to the New Brunswick Arts Board and the Canada Council for the Arts for their support while writing this book. Also to Don McKay and Tim Lilburn for herding chipmunks at the ten day Conversation and Silence: A Symposium on Writing and the Natural World held at St. Peter's College in 2001.

Notes on the Text

"Falling Angels" was inspired by *La chute des anges,1998,* twelve monoprints on paper by Herménégilde Chiasson. "Girl with Shell" is a response to Fred Ross's painting, *Girl with Shell.* Many of the details in "The Dwarf" were found in the photographs of Freeman Patterson in his book *Odysseys.* Jung Chang's book, *Wild Swans,* inspired some of the images in "The Map Maker."

In "The Time of Novels," the reference to Egdon Heath comes from Thomas Hardy's *The Return of the Native.* In the same poem, the reference to Merlin comes from *The Once and Future King,* by T.H. White. In "Driving West on the 116," the quotation comes from *Angle of Repose,* by Wallace Stegner.

"Vocation" is for Deannie Sullivan-Fraser. "Quartet" is for the members of the Leo Hayes High School String Quartet who played in the 2002 Fredericton Music Festival. "After Halftime" is in memory of Sarah Elizabeth McLain, 1989-2003.